Welcome Home

Ken Byerly   John Laughlin
Mike Moran   Steve Raho

THE PAPER HOUSE
PUBLISHING

CONTENTS

Paperback ISBN: 978-108-804-765-1

eBook ISBN: 978-108-804-780-4

This book is dedicated to our families. Without their untiring love and support, especially our wives – Jean, Karen, Pam, and Sheila – this book would never have become a reality. We love you all! And to the 58,281 (confirmed by the Vietnam Veterans Memorial Fund via the phone, 202 393-0090, on 11/23/21) names on the Wall...
you will never be forgotten.

To the Lucky Ones who made it back to the U.S:

WELCOME HOME!

INTRODUCTION

Well, here I go again, trying for the second time to author a book about Vietnam. The first attempt ended with three of the contributors pulling out. Trying to recall what happened to them in Vietnam was too painful... I understand and respect their decisions.

I determined to try again, this time with a different group of collaborators, all Vietnam Veterans and good friends: John Laughlin, Mike Moran, and Steve Raho.

This book is important. We want our families (and others) to understand why Dad, Mom, Grandpop, Grandmom, uncles, aunts, etc. act the way we do and why we don't talk much about their tour in Vietnam. With that in mind, the majority of this small volume will focus on both our in-country and coming home experiences. If you are reading this book and you are a Vietnam Veteran, you are – as a friend of mine, Army Colonel Tom Vossler, Ret. – says, one of the "Lucky Ones." We made it home. The contents of this small book contain statistics to support the claim.

Most importantly, I want my immediate family, especially Jean (my wife), my sons (Michael and Daniel), my grandchildren (Ian, Erin, Liam, and Genna), and my extended family, to know how much I love them. There's nothing I wouldn't do for them. Even though at times I may not show or speak it, you are my life.

I hope you find this book enjoyable and educational, without the blood and gore of some books on Vietnam. We want to provide readers with a different prospective to a dark time in our nation's history: race riots, anti-war protests, political assassinations at home, lack of support for the military, and an American population divided for and against the Vietnam War. Details of the events and activities in this book are true and real as endured by the memories and experiences of the author and the contributors to the best of their recollection. Where contributor information is used, the people are real. I use actual names only with the contributor's permission.

Pictures in the book were supplied by the author and/or the contributors. Some were obtained from other Veteran sources. Credit is given, where available. Some did not have a source for attribution, but their use in the book is important and conveys an impactful message.

And I am *The luckiest of the Lucky Ones!*

God bless you – and God bless America.

PROLOGUE

Why am I writing this book? Why us?

Vietnam Veterans are now in our late 60s or 70s or older? We are more than fifty years removed from our war experiences and I've decided to write about it now? Why? Why would you want to read it? I asked myself all those questions.

Over the years since the '60s and '70s, opportunities to talk about our experiences in Vietnam were minimal and, for some, often too painful to recall. But for some Vietnam Veterans, the war has never left. Lost limbs, horrendous scars, effects of Agent Orange (I am among this group), PTSD, etc. are some of the constant and recurring reminders of a horrible time. Some find the memories unbearable.

War, any war, takes its toll on the men and women who do fighting and/or support the grunts, infantry or foot soldiers, in a war zone.

This book talks about my experiences and those of several of my Vietnam Veteran comrades, three Army Veterans and one Air Force, who wanted to contribute their own feelings and/or incidents. The Air Force Veteran wasn't really "in-country," so he provides a different perspective of "fighting a war." Like a lot of Air Force and Navy Veterans who were not in-country, some were on the ground in Vietnam – the Black Ponies in the Mekong River Delta for example –

were still part of the overall war effort and subject to being wounded, captured or even losing their lives. When I recount their perspective, opinions, points of view or war experiences, I will use their real name and their first-hand experiences. We will attempt to explain what happened to each of us so that the American people, even those who lived through the Vietnam War years, have a better understanding of what we and our peers (brothers and sisters in uniform) went through and try to relate it to today.

How can I do that? As I said, it's been a long time. Times change. Different wars and types of enemies. Different countries. Different political situations. Different views on the war by the American people? But there is one constant in every war the United States has ever engaged in – the U.S. service person. Be it Army, Marine Corps, Air Force, Navy, or the Coast Guard...doesn't matter.

We want the people who read this book to understand the sacrifices made by the men and women in uniform and their families for this great country. However, the reader also needs to understand what is going on in 2022 as it relates to our young people returning from Iraq and Afghanistan. These are Veterans with traumatic brain injuries (TBI), post-traumatic stress disorder (PTSD), and enduring an appallingly high rate of suicides. They require...no, they have earned and deserve...care.

President John F. Kennedy once made the following statement about caring for our Veterans:

Let us not seek the Republican answer, or the Democratic answer, but the right answer.
Let us not seek to fix the blame for the past.
Let us accept our own responsibility for the future.

I am not a professional writer – just a concerned Vietnam Veteran who feels the reader needs a better understanding of the Vietnam Veteran and how he/she faces the challenges of the war. I also want to be the voice of all those Veterans who cannot or won't speak about their war experiences. Their stories must be told, and their stories must be heard.

In addition, there were some misconceptions about the Vietnam War then and they still exist today. Throughout the book, I will provide data that clearly demonstrates how each of these conceptions was misinterpreted by many Americans via a one-sided media explanation of the war, which resulted in a non-supportive attitude towards American troops.

One Vietnam was enough! Our Veterans deserve more...they've earned it. To each and every Veteran who reads this book, especially my Vietnam Veteran brothers and sisters...

WELCOME HOME
&
THANK YOU FOR YOUR SERVICE!

ONE

Before the Service, Entrance, and Basic Training

KEN

For many of us, the time before the service was fraught with worries about getting through high school and graduating, about getting drafted, going to college, getting married (some to avoid the draft), etc. Having grown up in Long Island, NY, my draft board, Freeport, allegedly had some of the highest numbers of guys getting drafted in the state of New York.

However, having gone to a military high school, many of my instructors impressed upon me the need to enter the service as an officer and not to get drafted or enlist. My plan was to go to a military college when I graduated high school. A few of my childhood friends got drafted, one had a hardship deferment to take care of his sisters due to their parents' deaths in a car accident, and some went to college.

The United States in the '60s and '70s was a country torn apart by:

- Civil rights unrest and riots.

- A public divided over the Vietnam War. Some felt it was necessary to offset Communist aggression in Southeast Asia;

others felt the war was a waste of young American lives, money and time. They let their feelings be known via rioting, avoiding the draft (conscientious objectors, deserters running away to Canada, etc.), anti-war protests, the Peace Movement, etc.

- Political assassinations:

    John F. Kennedy (assassinated on November 22, 1963)
    Martin Luther King (assassinated on April 4, 1968)
    Robert Kennedy (assassinated on June 5, 1968)

- For the first time in our nation's history, a war, the Vietnam War, was being televised almost nightly into the living rooms of American homes as a constant reminder.

- Political unrest and troubles in South Vietnam. Ngo Dinh Diem, a politician supported by the United States, was assassinated on November 2, 1963, by some of his generals. Buddhist monks set themselves on fire in protest of persecution by Diem's government.

- A country, South Vietnam, with corrupt political leadership and an unwillingness to defend its own people and territory or to support U.S. military personnel.

As a teenager, it was a tough time to be facing a lot of decisions that would affect your life – or take it in an unwanted direction. Sometimes things were out of your control the moment you graduated from high school. One of my friends and a contributor to the book, John Laughlin, went to college and decided to take a semester off. He was drafted. As you will read later, his decision to join the Army almost cost him his life. Another contributor, Mike Moran, tried to get into the Reserves or National Guard after graduation from La Salle College in Philadelphia, but his plan didn't happen. He received a pre-induction notice and decided to enlist – he wanted some sense of control of where he was going and with what branch of the service. He took the Air Force, Marine, and Navy officer program tests. He did really well on the Air Force exam, so he signed with the Air Force in their navigators program.

I grew up in Levittown, Long Island, NY, in a middle class family where both my parents worked. We were Irish/Dutch Catholics. My grandfather served in WW I; my father served in WWII. I had a sister five years older than me. I went to a military high school, so my plan was to go to a military college and enter the service as an officer.

It was a difficult decision to make at that time because the American public, in general, held the military in low esteem and was not supportive of our troops at all – or of the war. I entered Pennsylvania Military College (PMC) in the summer of 1964 as a Rook (freshman). The four years there were exciting with a lot of challenges both academically and militarily. Most importantly, PMC is where 1 met my best friend, future wife, and the mother of my two sons, Mike and Dan.

Upon graduation from PMC on May 26, 1968, I attended six weeks of basic training at Indiantown Gap in PA and received my commission as a "butter bar" – a second lieutenant. The training cadre at the Gap were members of the 82nd Airborne Division. Some of them had just returned from Vietnam; some were short timers – fewer than 30 days left in the service. This was my first experience talking to Vietnam Veterans. Some of their stories were exciting and interesting – others were outright scary.

Upon completion of summer camp, I returned to Philadelphia, married Jean, and got a job with an insurance company in Philadelphia. I was allowed a one-year deferment until I had to report to the Army, and I took full advantage of it.

During that year, Jean got pregnant. It was not planned at all, but we were happy. But we were also concerned, especially about the possibility of Vietnam in my immediate future. In June of 1969, I reported to Fort Eustis, VA, to begin my Transportation Officers Basic Course (TOBC), which lasted ten weeks. Then, I was sent to Fort Knox, KY, for a two- week advanced course in transporting tanks.

While in Ft. Eustis, Jean gave birth to our son Michael, who was born eight weeks premature but healthy. Before I left Ft. Eustis, I was told I would probably be in Vietnam in less than a year. They offered me a two-year stint in Germany after which I would go to Southeast Asia. The year was 1969. I opted for Germany. Once Michael turned 30 days old, we flew out of McGuire Air Force Base, NJ, to Mannheim, Germany, where we spent almost two years before I received orders for Vietnam.

My time in Germany was educational as an officer and fun for all of us. When I arrived at the 28th Transportation Battalion in Mannheim, Germany, I was assigned as a platoon leader in the 69th Transportation Company. My Commanding Officer (CO) and my First Sergeant (or Top as we called him) were great people who helped me acclimate to my new assignment.

I was at the 69th for only four months before I was reassigned as the Adjutant and Commanding Officer of the Headquarters and Headquarters Detachment, 28th Transportation Battalion in February 1970. I was promoted to First Lieutenant. I had approximately 125 people on the HHD staff under my command. I continued in the position until July 1971. In the late spring of 1971, Jean and I went on leave to Majorca, Spain. I told her I had received my orders for Vietnam – a difficult adjustment for both of us.

In 1967 while at PMC, the reality of the Vietnam War slapped me in the face hard and forced me to rethink my future plans. I was visiting my home in New York. I attended a viewing for a friend of mine, Walter's brother, Stephen Karopczyc. He'd been killed in action in Vietnam. He was twenty-three. I was in my PMC Cadet uniform and was going to return to school. I was with a friend who had been drafted. He was in his Army uniform and preparing to return to his base. The two of us had known Stephen's parents for around 10-15 years. We had gone to school with their sons and visited their house quite often.

Walter's mom walked up to us. "Who are you and why are you dressed like that?" she asked.

We were both twenty-one – and dumbfounded by the question. Walter came over and walked his mother back to his dad. He returned and apologized. We asked what was going on with his mother, an intelligent, beautiful woman with a great personality. Apparently, she had demanded to view her son's remains even though everyone advised against it. She was insistent until it was allowed.

She was not prepared for the extent of Steve's injuries – and she never fully recovered from the shock. Her son, Stephen Edward Karopczyc, would later be awarded the Medal of Honor for his heroism and bravery. (Details will come later.)

Before I went to the viewing, my future plans were to stay in the Army as a career and get out after 20 years, but Steve's death made me rethink. I was stationed in Germany for almost two years and returned home as a first lieutenant in August 1971. Before I left for Vietnam, I learned my fraternity big brother had been killed in action on March 23. I had lost two friends in two years.

I had a wife and son who was barely two years old. While I was deployed in Vietnam, Jean and our son lived with her parents, Frana and Sarge (my nicknames for them). I can never repay them for their love, devotion, and kindness. Words fail me – they took care of those dearest to me at a critical time.

§§

JOHN

John Laughlin was born in Philadelphia and then moved to Ocean City, NJ, and then returned to Levittown, PA, where he was raised and went to school. He was the only child of two working parents in a middle class family. Most of the families in Levittown were remarkably similar. They boasted Veteran males in the family and maintained a keen sense of patriotism and a determination to be law abiding. John learned the value of work from an early age and the importance of being economically independent.

His entrance into the service took a different path from mine. After his graduation from high school, John attended Rider University for one year and decided to take some time off – bad choice – he was drafted. His basic training and Advanced Infantry Training (AIT) were at Fort Hood, TX.

He secured a position as a company clerk in one of the battalions of the Second Armored Division. His first sergeant took him aside and told him he'd be getting orders for Vietnam in the near future. It was

October 1967. John had never thought much about Vietnam, but it got into his mind PDQ in '67 when he and his unit spent all of November and part of December in jungle training. He was given a two week leave before Christmas and told to report to Oakland, California, for indoctrination and additional training.

Here's a pic of Spec. 5 John Laughlin taken in December 1967 at Ft. Hood, TX, during jungle warfare training just before deployment to Vietnam. He's standing in front of an M6OA1 tank.

He received his vaccinations, camouflaged fatigues, and boots. John was there for three weeks and was never allowed to leave the base. He slept in a large auditorium with nothing but rows and rows of Army cots. Morale amongst the troops was not good due to the confinement and a lack of available recreation facilities. They had nothing to do but listen to the radio or write home. He said the food was typical Army: meat, potatoes, vegetables, milk and/or Kool-Aid. He was a draftee with less than one year in the Army; he never thought they would send him overseas. He had a two-year obligation; one was already gone.

A typical deployment to Vietnam was 13 months, so he figured he would serve out his last year at Ft. Hood training recruits as part of the cadre. Suddenly, his unit began to switch from motor pool duty to jungle warfare training and survival techniques. John had trained as an 11E20 (his Military Occupation Specialty, MOS). He was an armored vehicle (tank) crewman. After his additional training, however, his MOS reverted back to an 11 Bravo - an infantryman or "grunt" as we called them in Vietnam. In December 1967, he received orders to deploy to Vietnam in January 1968. As he and the other guys prepared to go to Vietnam, they were unaware of what was going on in America. They had no idea about widespread displeasure with the war.

Two weeks later after more training, John and his buddy were on an American Airlines plane on their way to Vietnam.

§§

MIKE

Mike Moran grew up in Bryn Mawr, PA, just outside of Philadelphia. Both his parents worked. His Dad was a postal clerk and his Mom worked as a medical records librarian. He had one sister who was ten years younger. He went to Catholic schools and graduated from La Salle College while working part-time jobs and playing basketball. Mike's Mom died after an extended illness in the summer after his freshman year. He stopped playing (he said he "retired from") basketball to take care of his sister after school. He worked and studied when his father got home.

In late January of 1968, Mike received job offers from HUD and the Pennsylvania Railroad. He asked his high school sweetheart to marry him, and she said yes. His future wife, Pam, was already working as a teacher in the local school district. They were married on June 22, 1968. Meanwhile, in Vietnam, the Tet Offensive erupted. Most guys in his college graduating class received pre-induction notices from their "friends" at the draft board. Mike wanted some control of his future in the military, so he started looking for officer candidate programs offered by the Navy and Air Force. The Marines were "just too nuts" in his words. The Air Force worked out.

After completing Air Force Officer Candidate School (OCS) at Lackland Air Force Base (AFB), his wife could join him wherever he was stationed. The only problem – he had to report five days after he was married. A funny aside: Mike had never flown before. He liked to say, "I got sick on Tilt-a-Whirl."

Mike completed OCS as a distinguished graduate at Lackland AFB in September 1968 and went to Mather AFB for ten months of navigator training. In June 1969, he chose bombardier training – another seven months. Mike had chosen the Strategic Air Command (SAC) and a B-52 slot. When Mike finished bomb school, he was off to survival school, POW training, and B-52 combat crew training at Castle AFB. He received orders for Ice Station Loring AFB in Maine and arrived in late September 1970. He was certified as combat ready in December 1970. Since entering the service, Mike's wife Pam had delivered two children and followed him from base to base.

Mike volunteered for an Arc Light tour (the Strategic Air Command's code name for a Southeast Asia Tour) and was assigned to a new, experienced crew in February 1971. Five months later, Mike arrived at Royal Thai Navy First Air Wing (RTNAS) in U-Tapao, Thailand. He flew his first mission three days later...targets were all in South Vietnam and Laos. His crew nickname at first was "Gator" or "Bombs." It was later upgraded to "Radar." Mike's tour in Southeast Asia had begun.

§§

STEVE

A classmate of mine from PMC, Steve Raho, was from Tower City,

PA, a small coal mining town that was mostly pro-military. He was never exposed to the anti-war sentiment. On the day we graduated from PMC, unbeknownst to Steve, he was considered to be on active duty. He reported to his first duty station as a mechanized platoon leader with the 5/6 Infantry Battalion, 1st Armored Division at Fort Hood, TX.

Since he worked six days a week at Fort Hood, he did not have time to mingle in the civilian community. The major concern of most of his civilian friends seemed to be worrying about their draft number and when it would be called. Steve served at Ft. Hood for about three months (as a mechanized platoon leader in the 1st Armored Division) and then went to Ft. Benning in Georgia for Infantry Officer Basic Course followed by Airborne School. Steve left Fort Benning in December of 1968 and returned to Ft. Hood for an abbreviated time. He was then sent to Jungle School in Panama in February/March of 1969 and from there to Vietnam, arriving in April. Steve was a second lieutenant when he arrived in country and was promoted to first lieutenant in the field around the first week in June.

As you can see, each of us took different directions into the service, our basic and advanced training, and our preparedness for Vietnam/Southeast Asia. There were many reasons why young men in the '60s and '70s did not want to go into the service. It was a challenging time to be in the military...any branch.

I wouldn't wear my uniform to church or out to a restaurant because of people's reactions. I endured name calling, dirty looks, and not so very friendly peace signs, and I hadn't even gone to Vietnam yet. People called me a woman/baby killer in reference to the My Lai massacre of March 16, 1968, and I hadn't left the States yet. During my leave from Germany and prior to going to Vietnam, I received orders promoting me to captain. The orders contained my next assignment: Phu Bai, Republic of South Vietnam.

One of the misconceptions about the Vietnam War then and even today, was that it was fought mostly by draftees, and they incurred the most casualties. Nothing could be further from the truth. Here are some statistics.[1]

- 25% (648,500) of total forces in country were draftees

- Draftees accounted for 30.4% (17,725) of combat deaths in Vietnam
- From 1965-73, total draftees = 1,728,344...38% of draftees served in Vietnam
- 66% of Vietnam Veterans volunteered

Consider my friends and me. Two were drafted, one of which decided to enlist to choose his own path. The two others enlisted due to an obligation via college ROTC.

Interesting, isn't it? There will be more quantifiable information in the pages to come, but now, off to Vietnam and Southeast Asia.

Two
In Country – or Over It

Let's describe the conditions in South Vietnam as seen through the eyes of Veterans of the war:

- The country was deplorable...hot, humid, rain soaked during the monsoon season 24/7, mosquito infested = malaria... little to no support from the Army of the Republic of Vietnam (ARVN)... a lot of them had no desire to defend their country...lack of training, lack of motivation and no sense of nationalism.
- In some areas, drug usage by the American troops was high...mostly marijuana and/or heroin.
- A lot of the troops were only 18, 19 or 20 years old (more on this later).
- Scariest times in country...first 30 days – new, don't realize what to be scared of or where the danger lies...last 30 days – develop a short-timer attitude and know all too well where not to go not to be and avoid any volunteering.

Our basic and advanced training completed, and our orders

received, it was time to board a plane and head off to Southeast Asia and the Republic of South Vietnam.

§§

KEN

Let me begin with my experience of flying out of Philadelphia in late August of 1971 and leaving my wife and two-year-old son with Jean's parents. It was a difficult, emotional time accompanied by the fear that I would never see them again. The emotions were overwhelming.

I flew to Ft. Lewis in Washington State and started processing to go to Vietnam almost immediately upon arrival. In a couple of days, I was on a Pan Am flight headed for Vietnam with a stop in Hawaii. We had a layover in Hawaii, so the crew could get rest. I asked if I could go out of the airport to get something to eat. Permission granted. I found a small bar/restaurant and went in. As I did, a rather large Hawaiian man came up to me and said I had to leave because my kind (in uniform) weren't welcome there. So I left and went back to the airport. It was a total disrespect of the uniform and the service...his loss. Back at the airport, the crew finished their required rest time and we left for Vietnam.

It was around 2:00 am when we began our approach to the airport in Cam Ranh Bay. Suddenly, the pilot veered the plane to one side to avoid what appeared to be an orange ball of flame coming up from the ground. We finally landed and went to a secure location to disembark the plane. We were directed to cement bunkers used to protect jet fighters and we were told the Viet Cong (VC), or the North Vietnamese Army (NVA) had just blown up an ammunition depot as we approached. A sergeant said, "Welcome to Vietnam."

I was only in Cam Ranh Bay overnight. I received orders to go to Phu Bai, which was north of Da Nang. I boarded a C-130. When I arrived in Da Nang, I was met by a Captain, Bill by name. We'd served together in Germany. On our Jeep ride back to his unit, I was introduced to the Vietnamese concept of "the cowboy." A Vietnamese teenager would jump in front of an American Jeep and make it stop. His pals would swarm the vehicle and try and steal everything not tied down or secured. They almost got my duffel bag, but I punched the guy in the face with so much force it chipped the stone in my college ring. (I never changed the stone). The guy I punched laughed and ran off.

Unfortunately, this was an omen of things to come for Bill. A couple of months later, Bill was driving a Jeep, accidentally hit one of the cowboys and injured him. Bill was taken hostage by some of the locals and put in a room with two unclipped hand grenades and an M16 taped around his neck until the U.S. paid compensation for the injured boy. Bill was held hostage for several hours but was safely released after the U.S. ransomed him. I never asked how much was paid.

Bill was physically unharmed, but the incident took its toll on him mentally. Too bad because he was a West Point graduate and a great officer.

The next day I took a C130 to Phu Bai, located between Da Nang on the south and Hue to the north. I was assigned as the S1 (Personnel Officer/Adjutant) to the 26th General Support Group, who supported the 101st Airborne in Camp Eagle (Phu Bai) and Camp Evans...farther north of Phu Bai. In Army terms, we were located in I Corps.

Militarily, South Vietnam was divided into four regions or Corps. ...I Corps in the north, II Corps in the middle, III Corps in the south, and IV Corps in the area surrounding Saigon. Our base was across Highway 1 from the 101st, and we were in contact with them on a daily basis. We supplied the 101st with almost every necessity to do their fighting. Depending on your source, it takes between seven and ten support personnel to equip one grunt.

Supporting one grunt:

- Food & Water
- Gas or POL
- Ammunition
- Graves and Registration
- Transportation: jeep, 2 1/2 ton (deuce and a half), 1/4 ton, etc.
- Uniforms, boots, hats, etc.
- Weapons and Ordnance: M1, M14, M16, M79 grenade launcher, 45mm, M60, etc.

LTC John Browne, a retired quartermaster officer who served in the U.S. Army and is a Vietnam Veteran, stated:

What most people don't understand is the functional and professional relationship amongst customers and providers within the tactical supply chain irrespective of the mission area. It could be Vietnam, Korea, Normandy, Iraq, or Afghanistan. A review of history bears out this fact. I believe this relationship at the time was approximately 15-20% warfighters and the rest combat support and combat service support.

My cot was right behind the wall with socks on it. That wall later was a life saver due to a fragging in the hooch to the left in the picture.

I was assigned to a Quonset hut or "hooch" with a first lieutenant who worked for me. The first few nights, I didn't get much sleep. The artillery units were firing from across the street and choppers were landing and taking off at a small airport behind our hooches. It took me several nights until I learned the different sounds artillery and mortar rounds made – outgoing (a woof or thump sound) and incoming (a whistling sound). The choppers taking off and landing were a constant and one of those things you just got used to. Slicks (UH-1), Loaches,

and Chinooks (CH-47) were always in the air. The occasional C-130 or
Cobra (attack helicopter) made an appearance.

*This was my Momma-san, Nguygen Thy Hoa. We
called her "Missy Wa." A diligent worker and single
mom, her husband was killed by the VC one night
when they entered her village. I would guess she was
in her 30s did not speak fluent English – just enough to
do her job. The night before I left, I gave her an old
Army fan that no one wanted...she was happy. The
next day she came in with a swollen face and nose and
a black eye. The VC had come into the village, taken
her fan, and beaten her for working for the Americans.
I don't know what happened to her. I assume she
didn't last long after the United States pulled out. God
bless Missy Wa!*

My Commanding Officer (CO), a full colonel, was a great man who I
respected immensely. He was strict but fair and didn't like BS. He was a
straight shooter and I like that in a leader. The Executive Officer, a lieutenant colonel, was his exact opposite, and I'll leave it there. Our S3 or
Operations Officer was a major and a great guy. All three were career officers on their second tour in Vietnam. We had multiple responsibilities as
we closed out the Big Red 1, leaving Quang Tri in the north, and began the
withdrawal of the 101st Airborne. There were numerous chopper flights
to Quang Tri, Tan My, Da Nang and other places too small to remember.

However, one flight to Quang Tri and back I'll never forget. It was
with the three officers I mentioned along with a Slick's crew: pilot, co-

pilot and two gunners. As we were returning from Quang Tri to Phu Bai, flying near the mountains, the Slick suddenly began to shake violently. I watched the pilot talk to the co-pilot and then to my CO. We had taken some ground fire in the tail section of the Slick (I found out about it later). The pilot auto rotated to a safe landing zone.

We slammed down on the ground.

As we got out of the Slick, an artillery officer, a lieutenant colonel, pulled up in a jeep and said we had to get out of the area fast. The pilot, co-pilot, and two gunners stayed with the chopper. They wanted to fix it so we could lift off. The LTC took us to an artillery HQ bunker (mostly underground and surrounded by sandbags). He told my CO we had to be out of there before dark or we'd have to stay. My CO told him that wasn't going to happen. He used his walkie talkie to check on the chopper's status. During my first few days in country, I had learned the following: the U.S. and the ARVN had control of the country during the day, but at night, the place was ruled by the NVA and the VC.

It was getting late – and dark. The walkie talkie buzzed. The pilot said we could lift off but couldn't get any higher than 30 to 50 feet. The CO said, "Let's go!"

As we got closer to the chopper, the crew was signaling to us to get on board as quickly as possible – then I saw why. Coming over the mountains ridge were NVA troops. As we lifted off and banked, we could hear the rounds hitting the chopper's underbelly. We made it back to Phu Bai with no injuries or casualties, except for the Slick. To this day, chopper pilots have all my respect and admiration. They risked their own lives and the lives of their crew, to take people out of dangerous situations and safely "home." Thank you all for your courage, bravery, selflessness and caring.

I salute you!

Slick returning from a mission. Look closely: a gunner and another GI sitting in the door opening

The 26th General Support Group worked very closely with the 101st Airborne and they provided us with our perimeter security for our base. Security was a platoon of grunts placed around our perimeter in fox holes and security towers. Their job was to keep sappers (NVA who were trained to go around barbed wire and booby traps, infiltrate a defensive area, inflict damage, and then leave) and other infiltrators away from the equipment, supplies, and/or hooches. I was in my second or third month in country when a young butter bar (second lieutenant) from the 101st told my sergeant first class (SFC) he wanted to speak to me. I agreed. He came into the hooch, saluted and introduced himself.

I thought, *Boy, oh boy, we have a live one here.*

He had recently graduated from West Point and was assigned to us as our infantry security platoon leader. I welcomed him and asked how I could help. He wanted to be transferred to a regular 101st Airborne Infantry unit so he could earn his Combat Infantry Badge (CIB). I told him that was out of my area of responsibility, but I would speak to my CO and get back to him. I spoke with my CO and explained the young lieutenant's request. My CO said he understood and would see what he could do. He pulled some strings and got the young man transferred to a rifle company as a platoon leader. About a month later, the kid showed up again. His glasses were held together by tape and his uniform was a mess, but he had a big smile.

His unit had been on patrol the night before and was caught in an ambush. No one was killed but a few of his men were wounded. He was on his way to the MASH unit to see them but wanted to stop by and thank me for his transfer. He had earned his CIB and couldn't have been happier. I said, "You're welcome."

Never saw or heard from him again. I hope he made it safely through his tour.

Security tower on our defensive perimeter. The only thing holding you from certain death was a not very secure chicken wire enclosure.

Behind our unit was a Military Police (MP) K9 unit with some of the largest German Shepherds I had ever seen. The MPs were constantly training with them in their compound. One day on the way to my hooch, I saw a young Vietnamese woman walking from a storage warehouse to the fence. Not really. She was counting her steps and making calculated turns from the warehouse to the fence and back. I called the MPs and described what I saw.

This pic is of the top of the security tower. You see a flak jacket, helmet, M16 with a starlight scope attached. With the scope, it made night a light green, and you could see images and objects as if they were lit up.

A few minutes later an MP handler with a dog approached her; she began to run...bad idea. The MP let the dog go. The woman got about five steps away before the gargantuan animal cornered her. The MP took her away.

Later in the day, the MP handler came and thanked me. The woman admitted being a VC sympathizer who was helping sappers zero in on specific targets when visibility was hindered, limited, or sometimes nonexistent. I was relieved. My hooch was not far from the warehouse.

One of the problems we dealt with daily was drug abuse amongst the troops, particularly in the two man fox holes on our defensive perimeter. Sappers (VC or NVA) would try to infiltrate the barbed wire and booby trapped obstacles almost every night. The word among the grunts was that heroin would heighten their sensitivity to sound. Every morning, the floors of the fox holes were littered with small capsules, "nickel and dime" vials of a pure form of heroin.

Defensive perimeter as seen climbing the security tower. Village in the background, and the open, cleaned out area as you get closer to the base. Concertina wire, trip flares and mines were set up to catch sappers trying to infiltrate the base at night.

One night our Group Executive Officer (XO), decided to do a "drug raid" using every officer in the Group. He assigned each of us an area to search along with a Non-Commissioned Officer (non-com). The results were quite revealing. The CO of our Headquarters Company was moving wet sandbags to look under a hooch when, viola! He found bags full of nickel and dime vials of heroin. When a real sandbag gets wet, it weighs about 30 to 40 pounds – tough to move. The bags containing the heroin were much lighter. He didn't know who was responsible, but he had a pretty good idea.

That night, I had my first experience with "fragging" – a term used in Vietnam to describe the use of a fragmentation grenade by friendly forces to inflict injury or to kill officers or non-commissioned personnel, sometimes due to disciplinary action. Our Sergeant Major had heard about the drug discovery and recommended the HQ CO sleep in a different hooch for the night. Thank God he did; the move probably saved his life.

Our hooches had sheet metal roofs. In the middle of the night, I heard what I thought was a rock or something hit the roof of the hooch next to mine – the one where the HQ CO normally slept. The sound wasn't normal, so I hit the floor. An explosion rocked my hooch. Shrapnel flew through the ceiling. Most of it landed in the wall outside my bunk. No one was hurt, but it was a scary situation.

There was another fragging incident involving a high-ranking NCO at another base in our Group. The NCO got out of his cot and stepped on a trip wire that set off a Claymore mine under his cot. He survived but lost both his legs at the knees. We later uncovered a disgruntled American soldier who worked for him was responsible. It's a sad thing to be in a country where you aren't wanted and have to be on constant alert for fear your fellow Americans would try to injure or kill you.

Unconscionable.

We began to plan for the withdrawal of the 101st from I Corps. The phase down required a lot of coordination and communication. One of the biggest concerns was the transportation of troops from either Camp Evans or Camp Eagle to Da Nang. As with any troop movement, be it by air or convoy over the Hai Van Pass, the troops' safety was always our first priority. We planned for a Chinook (CH-47) helicopter loaded with 44 men (and its crew) to go to Da Nang for processing prior to a flight home. The chopper did not show up in Da Nang at its planned time. We waited for an hour and then ordered an aerial search. We eventually found the Chinook on a mountainside, apparently shot down. We had to send in our Ordnance Unit because the wreckage and bodies had been booby trapped by the VC or NVA. Once the site was cleared, our Graves and Registration Unit went in with body bags.

There were no survivors.

Phu Bai, the village our Group was based in, had a saying about it that anyone who served there knew..."Phu Bai's all right!" It came from an NVA radio station who broadcasted...Quang Tri, a city to our far North, be careful, Hue, a city halfway to Quang Tri, be on alert, but Phu Bai's all right. We were not permitted to go to the village, but it appeared all the locals who worked at our base lived there. Most of the means of transportation for the locals were walking, bikes, mopeds or small buses.

I was there during monsoon season; it rained constantly. Everything was wet. The humidity was maxed; the place was crawling with mosquitoes, snakes, lizards, spiders, etc. Mosquito netting helped a little (and cut down on malaria), but as one guy put it, the mosquitoes were as big as B-52s, and they sounded like one. (A little bit of an exaggeration but a good descriptor.) It was always wise to turn your boots upside down and smack them against something hard before putting them on just in case there was an "unwanted visitor."

Most of the soldiers were young. Of the men killed in Vietnam, 61% were twenty-one-years old or younger. They served with distinction. Many came home with visible wounds. Others carried scars no one could see.

Our country was splitting apart into two extreme sides: anti-war protestors on the left and pro-war on the right. The returning Vietnam vets fell right in the middle.

*Believe it or not, this is Bob Hope and his troop at the "Eagle Bowl."
Look above the stage, and on the roof it says, "Screaming Eagles," a
reference to the 101st Airborne. In the background you see two
Chinooks, which transported Bob Hope and his people, s and a few
Cobras that provided escort.*

On a happier note, we got to see Bob Hope at the Eagle Bowl. Bob
and his troupe arrived via Chinooks accompanied by Cobra gunships.
His opening joke was about stepping off the chopper and sinking up to
his neck in the mud. Odd – even though it was the monsoon season, it
hadn't rained in 24 hours and the ground was dry. Since they were
taping the show, they had to reshoot the opening with new lines and a
better audience reaction. I give Mr. Hope and his crew credit though.
They could be at home enjoying themselves with their families and
friends, but they were in this hell hole trying to bring smiles and a little
bit of home to some tired and homesick soldiers.

God bless Bob Hope!

§§

JOHN

My friend John Laughlin had a similar welcoming experience when he arrived in Tam Ky, South Vietnam, in I Corp. It was home to the 23rd Infantry Division (Americal Division). The plane landed at around midnight; the airport was under enemy fire. He had to exit the plane quickly and waddle like a duck to a nearby armored plated bus. He said it looked like a converted school bus with bars on the windows and wrapped in some kind of armor.

Again, "Welcome to Vietnam."

The bus took him and the other new arrivals through the jungle for a ninety minute ride to a place called "Cigar Island" for more processing and to await their assignments. He was assigned to a tent for some sleep. He would complete processing the next day. He wasn't sure where this reception center was, but it was located close to a beach and a large body of water. He said it could've been the South China Sea, but he didn't know for sure.

John was trained as an armored vehicle (tank) crewman – a Military Occupation Specialty (MOS) 11E20. When he arrived in Vietnam he was a Spec 5 (or E5), but his MOS was reverted back to an 11B (grunt). At the reception area, the men practiced tactical maneuvers and attended classes on what to expect when they got to their assigned units.

A week later, John was on a helicopter to his new unit: Second Platoon, C Troop, 1-1 Cavalry, 23rd Infantry Division (Americal Division), which was headquartered in Chu Lai.

His first few days were spent getting acclimated to the base, affectionately known as "Hill 29." It was near Tam Ky. His living quarters was a large tent with 15-20 other men. There were no showers. But they did have outside latrines, a mess tent, and a lot of dirt. The guys in his platoon were mostly white, high school educated from working class neighborhoods from the northeast section of the US. The majority of them were draftees. About a third of them were regular Army. He went on patrols made up of six to eight guys plus an ARVN interpreter. They went during the day – not too far, maybe one click (one kilometer or 1,000 meters/3,280 feet) from the base camp. At night, they secured the camp. His mission was to secure the perimeter of the camp every day and night. Each patrol lasted anywhere from 45 minutes up to two hours. The camp would usually come under attack at night, but in most instances, they held the VC off. The TET Offensive was ramping up and he could feel the tension and uncertainty in everyone's actions. He didn't have enough water for showers except every three or four weeks when a tank truck came in for bathing. If he wasn't out on patrol during the day, he would clean his weapon, get his clothes washed, play cards, or listen to music.

John probably did five missions before the fateful night of March 9, 1968, at around 2200 hours (10:00 pm for you non-military readers). Hill 29 was under attack from an NVA unit. I will let John tell you what happened next.

During a night maneuver in early March, we were ambushed and came under fire around midnight. I took an AK-47 round to the right chest and right forearm. A few of my buddies carried me to the medic, who then took me to a landing zone (LZ) in the middle of a field and placed me on a stretcher on top of a red X to await a medical chopper. Laying (sic) there I was scared...not knowing if l would die or come under attack even further. A chaplain came and gave us what I thought were the last rites. After a short time l heard the *swish, swish* sound of the chopper coming and [saw] its spotlight overhead. It lowered as close as it could while two medics strapped me to its side, secured me outside because it was already filled with wounded and dead. I remained outside on the side bars and off it went slowly to the closest field hospital.

The doctors and nurses at the field hospital were fantastic. I remember shivering cold (must have been shock) and asking for some blankets while laying (sic) there as they took care of the most serious wounded first. A nurse came over and cut all my clothes off because they were soaked with blood and stuck to my body. Next thing I knew, they gave me a shot of something that took the pain away and I felt like I was floating two feet off the stretcher. They took me in for an X-ray and then surgery as I was surrounded by men, like me, fighting for their life and limb. The next thing l knew, I woke up in a ward filled with fellow casualties and it was a day later. I had a large bandage attached to my chest where the heart is, and I got really scared. I asked the nurse what it was, she laughed and undid the bandage and said the doctor left me with a souvenir (AK-47 bullet) that almost killed you. I felt relieved that the slug didn't hit my heart and best of all, [was] a unique souvenir of my experience. I was medevac'd out to a MASH unit in Chu Lai along with many casualties from our company. Surgery was performed and we stayed there for about one week. From there to a hospital in Guam and then Japan for evaluation, rehab, and follow-up surgery.

John recalls that the night the base came under attack; the gunfire hit them before they had a chance to get their weapons and retaliate. There were many wounded, around 25 that night, and unfortunately, one was Killed in Action (KIA). The attack on his company that night was part of an orchestrated TET Offensive – the bloodiest days and nights (as far as casualties and wounded) in the history of the war, as reported by the Department of Defense.

Please see the following article from The Philadelphia Enquirer, dated March 10, 1968, entitled: *Armor and Jets Kill 129 Reds in Attacks Near Da Nang Base*. The article recounts the battle of the day before – the one during which John was wounded. John's grandfather followed the Vietnam War very closely and saved the article for him. John and his wife Karen uncovered the actual article 53 years later while looking through some other memories. It was turning yellowish brown. Thanks for finding it and sharing it with us.

The Philadelphia Inquirer

PUBLIC LEDGER
AN INDEPENDENT NEWSPAPER FOR ALL THE PEOPLE

100 FEATURES
And World's Best
ROTOCOMICS

"TODAY" Magazine
in Colorgravure

SUNDAY MORNING, MARCH 16, 1969

FINAL CITY EDITION

SECTION 1

TWENTY CENTS

Armor and Jets Kill 129 Reds in Attacks Near Da Nang Base

SAIGON, March 10 (AP).—(Sunday)—U. S. infantrymen riding armored personnel carriers killed 129 Communists without suffering a single fatality in an all-day battle Saturday in the coastal lowlands, the U. S. Command reported. Dive-bombing jets and U. S. field guns blasted at a...

Map shows the area surrounding the U. S. Marine base at Khe Sanh, South Vietnam. Black arrows indicate Communist infiltration routes. The white arrow marks an American helicopter route. Americans-held hills are marked with U. S. Flags, Communist-held hills by starred emblems.

U. S. Armor and Jets Kill 129 Reds

38

who were always by his side. He was flown to Ft. Dix, NJ, in May, then was sent to Valley Forge General Hospital for two months of therapy and rehab. We'll catch up with John in *Coming Home*. I am proud to call John my friend and Vietnam brother.

Hooah!

§§

STEVE

This is Second Lieutenant Steve Raho as an Infantry Platoon Leader with the 82nd Airborne Division in the Iron Triangle in III Corps in 1969, getting ready to go out on patrol. His patrol's mission was to look for Viet Cong (VC) and the tunnels they were building to stash weapons and ammo that were being brought in from North Vietnam. This is the only picture he has of his Vietnam service... the rest were lost in a house fire.

Steve Raho's start of his tour was a little different from the rest of us. Upon arriving in-country, as soon as he finished some rudimentary acclimation training at a large base camp, he was deployed to the field as a platoon leader with A Company, 1/505th, Inf.,3rd Brigade, 82nd Airborne Division. He had a rude awakening on his first day in the field. A soldier walking in front of him stepped on a mine and blew up his leg. In Steve's own words: "What a start to my Vietnam tour!"

Steve had little contact with the ARVN units because most of his unit operations were small. His normal schedule was to go out just before dark to set up ambushes for the night. A normal team would be made up of nine men. They established a triangle formation with three soldiers at each corner of the ambush, frequently in rice patty dikes.

He would return to base camp at first light, grab some chow, get some rest, and then go out on patrol in the middle of the day. When there was still some daylight left, they would be back at the ambush site without giving away their intention (because they were always being watched by the not-so-friendly farmers). After dark, they would return and move undetected into their ambush location. Steve said the conditions were miserable: going to sleep in a dry rice paddy and waking up later in a huge mud puddle because a monsoon had moved in. In the morning, he returned to his company's location as did all of the platoons that were out on their nightly patrols. They got food, rested, cleaned up, and then went on daytime patrol. He rarely engaged directly with the VC or NVA in large scale firefights because they knew he had the advantage and could quickly bring a lot of firepower into the action. Most of his skirmishes were with squad size (10 or 11 men) elements that got caught in the ambushes.

During the day, their 60 mm mortars and booby traps were a constant danger. Steve operated in an area where there was heavy Air Force bombing activity. Inevitably, not all the munitions exploded as hoped. Unexploded "bouncing betty" munitions made excellent booby traps. The VC were very inventive in producing a variety of munitions that were devastating when soldiers stepped on them.

Steve said: "We made good use of helicopters during the day in what were referred to as "Eagle Flights." A string of UH-1s would descend on our position and pick up the members of the platoon and drop us off in an area of suspected enemy activity. We would do a quick sweep of an area and then be picked up and dropped off in another location. On average, we probably did three or four drop-off searches a day.

One of Steve's most vivid memories was when he was a platoon leader during one of his usual nine-man night ambush patrols. He and his men assumed their ambush position in a rice paddy dike. The VC set off a 122 mm rocket so close to their position, the sparks from the launch fell on them.

Steve's platoon was made up of a wide variety of men – a few college graduates but most of them were just unlucky guys whose draft number came up and they could not get a deferment. He also had some enlistees who decided to make the Army a career. A few of them were on their second tour in Vietnam.

His best guess – around 60% were draftees. He had a variety of ethnic groups in his unit – Hispanic, Black, White. Steve's platoon sergeant was the best soldier he had ever known. Unfortunately, the man lost his life along with two other soldiers while trying to disarm a booby trap.

Steve has told me he still has flashbacks of some of these events. He has never really shared them except with me and a couple of others. Vietnam Veterans, especially grunts like Steve and John, have been through "living hells." It's hard to explain the situations to people you love because they don't or can't understand – they can't relate. A fellow Vietnam Veteran can. I belong to The American Legion Post 524 in Ocean City, NJ, and there's an old wives' tale about combat veterans from any war. If a visitor to the Post is looking for real, true war stories, look for the guy sitting at the bar by himself or eating alone. He'll have them.

Steve spent the first six months of his tour as a rifle platoon leader, A Company, 1/505 Infantry Battalion, 3rd Brigade, 82nd Airborne Division. During his tour, Steve's platoon participated in a wide variety of missions. They were engaged in combat operations in an area referred to as the Iron Triangle, which for many years had been considered a VC stronghold and virtually impenetrable because of its extensive network of trails and tunnels. His unit's area of operations extended to the Cambodian border including locations with names such as Hobo Woods, Angels Wing, and Parrots Peak. His missions included preventing the incursion of NVA and VC into the area surrounding Saigon which was referred to as the "rocket belt," an area close enough to the capital city to allow the VC to launch rocket attacks on military facilities, government buildings, the airport, etc.

The Mobile Riverine Force (MRF) was a unique Army-Navy strike force in the Mekong Delta of Vietnam. Steve's platoon participated in Riverine warfare operations.

Steve's unit was assigned to prevent another TET type surprise offensive on Saigon and included thwarting small unit and individual attacks by VC and sappers on vital supply lines (roads and bridges). His platoon also participated in Riverine warfare operations as part of a joint Army-Navy strike force established to conduct search and destroy operations along rivers and canals in the Mekong Delta.

Midway through his tour, Steve was selected to be an aide to the Commanding General, 3rd Brigade. It was interesting to see the war from a totally unique perspective. As a rifle platoon leader, he slept in the rice paddies almost every night. His sole concern was keeping his men safe and alive to perform their mission. He was constantly aware of the immediate dangers of ambushes, snipers, boobytraps, etc., and he had no time to think beyond that or how what he was doing fit into the overall picture.

As an aide, Steve caught a broader perspective. He traveled daily with the Commanding General (CG), primarily by helicopter, and visited the battalions at their field positions. He was briefed on their ongoing operations. Some of the trips also included visiting ARVN units. He attended daily briefings at the Brigade HQ at 1800 hours, where each section of the Brigade Staff, S1, S2, S3, S4, etc., addressed events of the day as they affected their functional area. The daily briefings in conjunction with his personal visits to the field units, were a very professionally rewarding experience for Steve because they allowed him to see the war from two sides – as "grunt officer" and as a staff officer.

Every Sunday (mission permitting), the Brigade Sergeant Major and Steve accompanied the CG on visits to hospitals where the seriously wounded were being cared for and stabilized prior to being Medivaced to an out-of-country facility for long-term care. It was an emotionally draining experience for Steve not just because it was sad to see the extent of some of the injuries but also because it was not unusual to find out that some of those they had visited a couple of days earlier had died while awaiting extraction.

§§

MIKE

Mike Moran wasn't in-country but over it in a B-52 bomber flying out of U-Tapao, Thailand in 1971. He flew his first mission three days after he arrived in July. B-52 tours lasted between five and six months; each mission was three to four hours. His targets were in all of South Vietnam and Laos.

A B-52 crew was made up of the aircraft commander (AC), co-pilot, radar navigator (bombardier), navigator, electronic warfare officer (EWO), and a gunner. The AC was usually a captain (up to a lieutenant colonel) with at least 1500 hours in the aircraft. The co-pilot was a second or first lieutenant with less than 1000 hours. The radar navigator was a captain through a lieutenant colonel with over 1500 hours – the EWO was a first lieutenant through a major with 500 hours. The gunner was usually a staff sergeant up to a senior master sergeant with anywhere from 100 to 5000 hours in the aircraft. The AC ran the crew, did most of the flying, and served as a mentor for the co-pilot. The co-pilot ran the aircraft systems, i.e., fuel, hydraulics, electrical, engine management, and radios. The radar navigator was the weapons manager and aimed the bombs. The navigator got the plane where it was supposed to be, helped with weapons, and managed time. There were always time requirements – refueling time, time over target, penetration times, etc. The EWO operated electronic radar jammers, hid the plane from the enemy, and, as a qualified navigator, assisted with celestial navigation. At that time, most B-52s were of two models...D and G. In the D, the gunner was in the tail with no ejection seat, a radar scope, and four, 50 caliber machine guns in a turret with windows. Serving as the gunner was a physically demanding job. The small, confined space bounced constantly. In the G model, the gunner was in the forward crew compartment with television and radar control of the guns...no windows.

U-Tapao, Thailand, was 80 miles south of Bangkok on the Gulf of Siam. Mike flew four-to-five hours-long missions three to five days in a row, then had two days off. Most of his missions were in support of ARVNs. He did some work around Special Forces camps in the Highlands and Laos. On one mission, the plane flew straight North in Thailand. They entered the timing box flying in an orbit (or circular pattern) when they received a call. An ARVN Special Forces camp was being attacked near the South Vietnam/Cambodian border. It was night. Three B-52s were releasing their bombs in "the wire" – an area measuring 750 yards by one mile. When the B-52s returned to base, they were informed the run accounted for 400 dead NVA. On another mission over Laos, his plane returned to base with close to 100 bullet holes in the tail. Mike said they didn't even know they'd been hit. He made captain, received a regular commission, and got home in October of '71.

When he arrived at Loring AFB in Maine, his family was there to greet him. To quote Mike, "The kids didn't know who the hell I was. They were two and three years old."

B-52 – Flew in a three plane cell.

When Mike returned stateside, he became a navigator instructor. His crew worked with Boeing engineers on a new cruise missile for the B-52 and was on nuclear alert for two weeks every month. In his words, "Life was good."

C-5 Galaxy delivering engines to Anderson AFB in Guam.

B-52 G models... Anderson AFB, Guam.

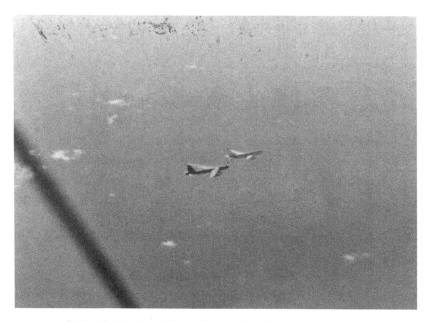

B-52 refueling from KC-135 Tanker from Clark AFB, Philipines.

View of B-52 cell (formation – which would include a code name) from
#3 plane thru cockpit window.

In May of '72, North Vietnam invaded the South. Over 120 G models and 30 D B-52s were sent to Guam for Linebacker I missions. Mike received orders for Guam and was assigned to a new crew. He arrived in Guam on November 1, 1972, and was in the air two days later. He said he felt uncomfortable because B-52 crews worked on trust and confidence in each other – sentiments that took a few weeks to build. On December 16, the B-52 crews were restricted to base. Mike knew something was up.

On the afternoon of December 17, 1972, 100 crews were called into a large briefing room. The briefing officer on stage was solemn. "Tonight, your target is Hanoi." Mike said all the air left the room. B-52s never went north. The mission was scheduled to last twenty-three hours and would require three refueling situations. Mike's plane would be the last one over the targets – fifteen minutes before sunrise.

Mike said, "Good thing the chaplain was right outside the briefing."

He flew missions on the first, the fifth, and the eight nights of Line-backer I. He was exhausted. SAC called the mission "The Eleven Day War." It stretched from December 19 until the 31st and involved 820 sorties.

The first night, they lost three airplanes, a D and two Gs. There were no losses on the second night. The third night was deadly: four Gs and Two Ds. In all, seventeen planes were destroyed, and fifty-six crew members were captured during the raids. The crew he had flown with in the previous year was hit. Fortunately, the plane limped back to Thailand. They all bailed out and were recovered. Hanoi had more air defenses, SAMs, and guns than Moscow. There were also MiG fighters.

Over the next week they only lost six more planes over the targets. Two more crashed and burned on landing due to battle damage – only one guy got out. Four more planes would never fly again but got their crews home. In North Vietnam, their targets were infrastructure, rail yards, power plants, MiG bases, SAM sites and Haiphong Harbor. Mike also bombed Radio Hanoi.

For Mike and his crew, the thought of being hit by the SAMs or MiGs was terrifying. Both the bombardier and the navigator positions were located in what the crew called the "Black Hole" – no windows. On the first night, 320 SAMs were fired at their plane with only three hits. The approach to North Vietnam took the B-52s down the same direction as the F-105s. It was called "Thud Ridge" – named for the sound a jet made when it crashed. When I asked Mike why anyone would send the B-52s down such a deadly path, he had no answer.

Mike Moran pulling pins from 750 pound bombs on a B-52 'D' model in U-Tapao, Thailand, in 1971.

He said all mission plans came from SAC in Omaha, NE. Go figure. Because the B-52s flew in groups of three, when a plane was hit, the co-pilot was responsible for communication. When a crew was ordered to eject, each crew member had a "beeper," which broadcast over "Guard Channel" and signaled a bailout. The most horrific thing to hear was the sound of the locator beacons going off as each crew member ejected from the plane.

I asked Mike how he and his crew mates knew what was going on in Vietnam. They were stationed in Thailand or Guam. He said most of the information came as part of the briefing before a mission. In Guam, they had the Armed Forces Network (AFN) or the BBC radio network out of Singapore. Sometimes they could get news coming out of Australia via the aircraft radios.

Mike's plans to make the Air Force a career started to change. Peace accords were signed in the end of January 1973. They had an end of the war blow-out party in Guam but continued flying missions in Laos and Cambodia thru March and April of '73.

§§

KEN

For me, Vietnam was a tragic place...not only for those in combat situations but also for some of the young men serving in country. I had one incident when a jeep came to my hut with a young soldier about 18 years old. The Gl had just arrived in Phu Bai from Cam Ranh Bay. He was covered with bumps all over his exposed body parts. When he arrived in Cam Ranh, there were no hooches available, so all the new arrivals had to sleep on the beach without mosquito netting. Unfortunately, the young man was allergic to mosquito bites – his medical record was clear about it. I had never seen so many bites and such swelling in my life. I sent him to our MASH unit where they treated him as best they could and then arranged for him to be sent home immediately. My question was, how did he even get to Vietnam in the first place? How was his allergy not uncovered during his in country processing in Cam Ranh?

A more tragic and sadder incident occurred one evening as I was working on plans to out process soldiers from the 101st Airborne in Phu Bai. In the hut next to mine, the guard detail for the night was getting their orders when a shot rang out. I grabbed my helmet, my flak jacket, and my .45 and started to run to the bunker. The Officer of the Day said everything was under control; I asked what had happened. I accompanied him to the guard hooch. There was a body – a young GI, about 18 or 19 years old. He was lying on the floor. The back of his head was smeared on the ceiling. There was a piece of paper in his hand.

He'd gotten a "Dear John" letter from his girlfriend back in the States. She was sorry, but she was going to marry his best friend. He put his chin on the end of the barrel of his M16 and pulled the trigger. So young – and for what? In a war, far from home, there was nothing he could do; the news was too much to bear.

Some people feel suicide indicates a personality flaw – something that would have come out later in his life. Maybe, but if he had been home in the States versus Vietnam, he could've attempted to resolve the issue by talking to his girlfriend. Even if she still left him, he would have lived a lot longer. But we'll never know. It was a senseless loss of life. And there were too many – too many who were too young who never made it home to become fathers, mothers, uncles, aunts, grandparents, girlfriends...That will be the subject of my next section, "The Vietnam Wall."

THREE
THE VIETNAM WALL

If you haven't seen The Wall, you should. If you haven't supported it, you should. There is one incredible – and disturbing – number: 58,281. Having graduated from high school in 1964 and college in 1968, I have many friends who were either drafted or enlisted – their names are on The Wall. They never returned to the States to have families, a career, continue their education, relish their lives, and spend each day with joy and happiness, etc.

I got my information on The Wall from several places.

- *The VVA Veteran Magazine,* May/June 2021. *Accounting For the Dead... The Wall and Shifting Casualty Classifications* by Marc Leepson
- Vietnam Veterans Memorial Fund
- The Vietnam Veterans of America (VSO)
- *The Veterans Hour* – Vietnam War Statistics
- *Vietnam War Statistics* – Statistic Brain

There are some amazing facts about the names and people on The Wall. This information should be shared in every classroom in this great country. I will attempt to share as much as possible. I want you to get the real impact of the Vietnam War on Vietnam Veterans when they returned home.

§§

Vietnam Wall history most people will never know.

- The first known casualty was Richard B. Fitzgibbon, of North Weymouth, Mass, listed by the U.S. Department of Defense as having been killed on June 8, 1956. His name is listed on The Wall with that of his son, Marine Corps Lance Corporal Richard B. Fitzgibbon III, who was killed on September 7,1965.
- 39,996 on The Wall were 22 years old or younger.
- The largest age group, 33,103, were 18 years old.
- 8,283 were just 19 years old.
- 12 soldiers on The Wall were 17 years old.
- 5 soldiers were 16 years old.
- One soldier, PFC Dan Bullock, was 15 years old.
- 997 soldiers were killed on their first day in Vietnam.
- 1,448 soldiers were killed on their last day in Vietnam.
- 31 sets of brothers are on The Wall.
- 31 sets of parents lost two of their sons.
- 8 women are on The Wall. They were nursing the wounded.
- The most casualties for a single day occurred on January 31, 1968: 245.
- The most casualties for a single month were May 1968: 2,415.
- West Virginia had the highest casualty rate per capita in the nation – 711 West Virginians are on The Wall.
- There are three sets of fathers and sons on The Wall.
- 54 soldiers attended Thomas Edison High School in Philadelphia.
- There are 160 Medal of Honor recipients on The Wall.

A recent article by Marc Leepson in *The VVA Veteran Magazine*

(May/June 2021) entitled *Accounting For The Dead...The Wall and Shifting Casualty Classifications* looks at the names on The Wall in a unique way. He writes: "The actual number of Vietnam War KIAs – service members who were killed in action, including those who subsequently died of their combat wounds – is 47,434." His figure is below the official count of 58,281 American soldiers, sailors, airmen, Marines and Coast Guardsmen who lost their lives in Vietnam during the war. In my opinion, if they served and died in Vietnam (for whatever the reason), they earned the right to be on The Wall.

Here are the other two misconceptions about the Vietnam War: The War was fought by *uneducated people* who were *poorer* than the average American. In truth, 79% of the men who served in Vietnam had a high school education or better when they entered the military service. This figure stands in stark contrast to the statistics from the Korean War (63%) and WWII (45%).

And, the War was not fought mostly by minorities. Of those serving in Vietnam, 88.4% were Caucasian, 10.6% were Black, and 1% were of other races.

FOUR

COMING HOME

KEN

For me, leaving Vietnam was, in an understatement, unbelievable! In February of 1972, I took a Slick from Phu Bai down to Da Nang to out process and then got on a plane for the good old USA. The process was simple and fast, and then we were assigned a flight. I had the next one out. We boarded the plane with all the excitement and anticipation of getting home safely and back to our loved ones. It was a commercial flight with female flight attendants. That was great for all concerned. Just before the plane was to take off, the flight attendants sat in their seats, nervous about what was coming. As the plane lifted off the ground, the sound of cheering, yelling, and victorious cursing was deafening. We were leaving on a jet plane...

...thank God!

The route back took us to Japan and then Alaska. When we left Vietnam it was probably 100 degrees with a high humidity. We landed in Anchorage; there was snow and ice everywhere. The plane taxied to a special building – the plane began to slide due to ice. Not too far from the gate, the tires hit a dry spot. We lurched to a stop and were told we had to deplane. The gate could not stretch far enough. We had to go outside.

My first thought...*You can't be serious.* We were wearing summer khakis with no field jackets; the outside temperature was well below freezing. It was *cold,* but we had survived much worse. We made it to the terminal. The next stop was Fort Lewis, WA, where we began our out processing. No one had slept. A Women's Army Corps Personnel Officer (WAC S1) – a lieutenant gave me my DD214 and explained my Veteran benefits.

"Have a nice life."

One funny thing. I was traveling with a friend named Bill, Operations Officer (S3) from my unit in Vietnam. He lived in the Seattle area. He said he would accompany me to the airport where his brother would pick him up. Great! As Bill and I were sitting near my gate (you could do that in those days), I saw a long haired hippie with a stringy beard that reached his waist. He was wearing a "Ban the Bomb" necklace and dressed like a flower child. When he started coming toward us, I thought, *Oh no, this isn't going to be good.* Bill saw the guy, jumped up, ran over, and gave him a hug. It was his twin brother.

Both men were big guys. I wish I'd had a camera. The photo would have been priceless. Bill introduced his brother, a conscientious objector who had fled to Canada to avoid the draft but returned back to the States to face his punishment, which was community service. We parted ways. I never saw Bill again, but I hope he and his brother lived happy, healthy, and full lives.

My flight to Philadelphia was aboard a 747, a fascinating plane. The flight was full; there were a lot of military types on their way home. I befriended a sergeant (E5) who lived in northeast Philadelphia. He was really excited to see his family. He had spent his entire year in Vietnam as a grunt and had seen a lot of action. When we landed in Philadelphia and deplaned, a flight attendant handed him a note from his parents. They were both working. He was to take a cab home.

Welcome home, huh?

I offered to give him a ride, but he refused. Waiting for me was my wife, her parents, and my two-year-old son. You will never find a happier man anywhere. Thank God I made it back to my family safe and sound.

I went back to my old company where I had worked before I left for the service. They guaranteed a job to any returning member of the military. Not a single guy at the company had served. They were still doing the same jobs they'd had when I left. I felt like the odd man out.

I decided to look for new work – and that's when the trouble started. During either phone or in person interviews, I would be called a "baby killer" (in reference to the My Lai Massacre), a "gook killer," a warmonger, or other nice comments. At one point, the interviewer suggested that I should take my service time off my resume. I asked him how would I explain the three year gap on my resume? He said anything would be better than telling people I had been in the Army, I was shocked.

I left it on.

The majority of the interviewers never asked me a single question about my service in Germany or Vietnam or about my rank or my Bronze Star. Either they didn't care or didn't want to show their ignorance of the military since they had not served.

I was finally hired by a man who appreciated my time in the service and acknowledged my successes in rank and my medal. I spent the next twenty-one years at the company and was extremely successful thanks to a man who accepted me for who I was and appreciated my experience as a Veteran. He took a chance on me.

Thanks, Artie!

Coming home was a rude awakening for most Vietnam Veterans. One Sunday after I got home; I went to church with my family. I saw a guy in uniform being mocked by people; I was shocked. The antiwar movement was still strong and anyone in uniform was a target. It didn't matter if you served in Vietnam or stateside, you were in uniform and you were the "enemy." The American public did not support the returning Vietnam Veterans and many of them wound up homeless, unemployed, alcoholics, drug users, or in jail. It was a shameful way to treat people who sacrificed a great deal by serving his/her country – often at the expense of their families. The VA was ill-equipped to manage the rising number of PTSD cases. They referred to those issues as "flashbacks." It was difficult to talk about the war with anyone except fellow Vietnam Veterans.

At that time, joining a VSO (Veterans Service Organization...American Legion, VFW, etc.) was the last thing on my mind. My family was first. A career and earning money were my priorities (and they are still important). But now, I am a member of The American Legion and a life member of The Vietnam Veterans of America. I am working on getting Veterans care for PTSD and TBI and trying to find ways to reduce homelessness and the high suicide rates amongst Veterans. Even in 2022, the VA is not properly manned or equipped to manage these cases effectively...sad.

As a friend of mine once told me, "Just because you don't agree with the politics at that time, don't take it out on the military. They were just doing their job and could have lost their life for your freedom."

§§

JOHN

John Laughlin stated that coming home was almost worse than going to Vietnam – imagine. Because he was a Purple Heart recipient and wounded, he returned to the U.S. via Fort Dix, NJ, and the Valley Forge General Hospital circuit. His only contact was with Army doctors and nurses. However, when he returned to duty at Fort Hood, TX, in late June of 1968, he encountered a lack of interaction with the public. He said he felt "invisible." Even though he wore a uniform and stood out, people would not look at him. Very few people would talk to him.

When it was time for his Expiration of Term of Service (ETS) from Ft. Hood on October 23, 1968, he had to take a commercial flight home to Philadelphia. John flew in his uniform to get the cheaper stand-by rate. The people at the airport in Texas were nice and supported the military, but that all changed when he arrived in Philadelphia.

There was no one there to greet him. John felt ignored and unappreciated. People gave him dirty looks. No one engaged him in conversation or took the extra step to say hello or thank him for his service. Both his parents worked. His father couldn't get off and his mother didn't drive. They said they couldn't come to the airport to pick him up and told him to take the train to Levittown, PA.

John stood in the aisle the entire trip. No one offered their seat to him; no one even made eye contact. When John arrived in Levittown, he had to walk one-and-a-half miles carrying his duffel bag. No one offered a ride. When he finally got home, the only living thing to greet him was his German shepherd, Otto. John said Otto would not stop licking him and jumping all over him. He felt his dog's greeting made up for the lack of welcome expressed by the citizenry.

John changed into his civilian clothing. He packed his uniform away in his duffel bag. He did not look at it for an exceptionally long time.

When John went out in public, many people didn't know what to say to him or how to ask questions about Vietnam...so they didn't. John said the most curious people were the kids in the neighborhood. They wanted to know how many "gooks" he killed or asked him to see his bullet wounds. As John said, at least they showed some interest.

John said that most of the American people were against the Vietnam War, and it appeared they were taking it out on Veterans. He has no hard feelings towards those people, just an immense thanksgiving for coming out alive and, for the most part, mentally unscathed. As John stated to me, "My love and deepest respect for all those who didn't."

Here is John Laughlin at 77 years old, still has the bullet the doctors took out of him. Truly a lucky one... Hooah!

§§

STEVE

Steve Raho's route home was very much different from the rest because he was a career military officer. He redeployed from Long Binh AFB in Vietnam as a first lieutenant aboard a C-141 aircraft with troops from the 3rd Brigade of the 82nd Airborne in December of 1969. They flew directly to Ft. Bragg, NC, and landed in Pope AFB where the reception and welcome home ceremony were quite impressive. When the ceremony was over, he got on a bus to take them to the commercial airport in Fayetteville, NC. From there, he took a flight to Harrisburg, PA. The flight had several stops. He doesn't recall any negative encounters on his way home.

Steve took a couple of weeks of leave before he reported to Fixed Wing Flight School at Ft. Stewart, GA, in January 1970. While on leave in his small town of Tower City, PA, he ran into the father of a friend who had been killed in Vietnam. The father was nice – the situation was not negative, just uncomfortable. Steve also saw several of his high school classmates who had served in Vietnam. They had cordial conversations. Most of the friends served out their draft obligations and exited the military. The majority who had remained in uniform were in the Air Force.

Steve knew the anti-war atmosphere in the U.S. was widespread. Opportunities to talk about his war experiences were few and far between. Even to this day, most Vietnam Veterans are reluctant to discuss the war except with colleagues... especially after a few beers. Talking to non-Vietnam Veterans? "They just wouldn't understand." How do you explain to someone who was not there and didn't have the same experiences as you, their minds tainted by the anti-war media always focused on the negative stories? Steve felt that if he explained what happened to him, it might appear he was boasting about his ordeal or looking for sympathy.

Veterans who were not in Vietnam had no frame of reference, so it was easier for them to avoid any conversation about the Vietnam War. Even talking to family members was difficult. Steve felt what he experienced in Vietnam was highly personal. Again, "They just wouldn't understand."

Being a grunt officer, Steve had strong feelings about the men he commanded and served with in Vietnam, he stated:

It would be helpful for folks to understand that although this was a very unpopular war being fought largely by teenage draftees who had no desire to be there...they fought heroically and in 99% of the situations, they did themselves proud. As is always the case with soldiers, they complained and bitched and moaned about their situations, but they still did everything they were asked to do.

Steve had a fulfilling, highly decorated thirty year career in the Army and retired as a full colonel. When Steve shared some stories of the combat action he and his men had seen in Vietnam, he told me I was the *second* person he'd ever talked to about it – in almost *fifty years*.

Unbelievable to carry such a burden alone.

I always remember the quotation from a Veterans' organization. It explains a great deal.

> *Not everyone who lost his life in Vietnam died there,*
> *Not everyone who came home from Vietnam ever left*
> *there.*

Thanks, Steve, for sharing your war combat experiences with me. At our next class reunion, let's toast all those who never made it home and to us "Lucky Ones" who survived to tell our and their stories.

Hooah!

§§

MIKE

Mike Moran had several treks from his multiple deployments in Southeast Asia where he served as a crew member in a B-52. I thought the Army was bad with acronyms, but the Air Force has them beat. Mike said when a B-52 crew was deployed, the service personnel were sent as a Temporary Duty Assignment (TDY) but received no credit for a Southeast Asia tour. He explained each deployment was for five to six months because – get this – if the crew changed to another Air Force Command, their records would show no Southeast Asia assignment and they would be eligible for one...crazy. Mike had a good friend who was transferred to Tactical Air Command and deployed on an AC-130 gunship in early 1973. His friend had already flown over 200 KC-135 tanker missions in Southeast Asia. His plane was the last Air Force plane shot down in the Vietnam War somewhere over Laos in February 1973. His remains were eventually recovered in the early 2000s. His family had a long wait for some closure.

In June of 1971, Mike was assigned to the U-Tapao Naval Air Base in Thailand. From there, he flew 54 missions over South Vietnam and a few to Laos, mostly in support of ARVN ground units and trail missions. (The Ho Chi Minh Trail was a major supply route running from North Vietnam through Laos and Cambodia to South Vietnam.) He returned to the U.S. in October of 1971. His family met his plane at the base. He was put on a special project for Boeing, which ran until June of '72. In October of '72, Mike was assigned to a new B-52 crew as a bombardier-navigator and received orders to deploy to Guam. While in Guam, he flew 48 combat missions over North and South Vietnam, Laos, and Cambodia. He returned to the U.S. in late May '73. Again, his family greeted him. In July '73, he went back to Guam where he immediately put in his discharge papers. He flew to Guam where he spent thirty-seven days flying training missions. He liked to say he was "bombing Iwo Jima."

Mike was required to be back in the U.S. for thirty days before he could be discharged. He was supposed to take a SAC courier flight to Maine, but the flight was canceled. He took a commercial flight to Presque Isle, Maine, through Boston. The previous two times he came home he flew directly to his base. Now, he was in a different world, so to speak. Here's how he explains it.

> "I was in uniform, carrying my duffel, B-4 flight bag and my helmet bag, along with a great tan. A gaggle of people were in the gate waiting area, and all conversation stopped when I arrived. Most uncomfortable and longest 45-minute flight of my life."

Mike, like the rest of us, felt uncomfortable in his own country...no respect for the uniform, no respect for the service to our country, no real "welcome home" or "thanks for your service." People avoided him. As John Laughlin put it, Mike was "invisible."

Mike feels strongly that the Vietnam War was a waste of human life and treasure and has a profound lack of respect for politicians in our country. Mike continues. "Had they (the politicians) had the fortitude and courage of our country's military, the war would have been over in '67." Well said and probably accurate and correct.

Mike spent five years, five months and fifteen days, 6/28/68-10/5/73, in the regular Air Force serving his country. He went into the service as a second lieutenant and was discharged as a decorated captain. He had served in multiple AFBs in Southeast Asia and the United States.

The four of us all agree we were some of the Lucky Ones. Still, we were home with our family and friends but dealing with people who were against the war and wouldn't let us forget it. There are 58,281 names on The Wall. How many of them are there because others said "no" to serving in the military due to dodging the draft, using deferments, claiming CO status, or leaning on religious beliefs?

Let me share a personal story of one young man on The Wall that affected my life through his sacrifice, heroism, sense of patriotism, and his dedication to the men who fought beside and with him. I wrote about him in Chapter 1 (attending the viewing). His service in Vietnam was exemplary and I want to share it with you.

My friend, First Lieutenant Stephen Karopczyc, was not one of us Lucky Ones. His body arrived at Dover Air Force base in Delaware and was later transported to the funeral home in Levittown, Long Island, NY. He and I had grown up in the same area of Levittown/Bethpage, Long Island, NY, but I was closer in age to his younger brother, Walter. We used to hang out at their house. His mom made some fantastic Polish dishes, especially around the Holidays. His dad was in upper management at Pan Am Airlines in New York City. His mother was a beautiful and intelligent woman. I think she had won some beauty contests in the early '40s. The Karopczyc's were Catholics and attended the same church as my family – St. Martin of Tours in Bethpage. Steve attended and graduated from a Catholic high school, Chaminade, in Mineola. He went to Springhill College in Mobile, Alabama, where he was in their ROTC program. Upon graduation he was commissioned as a second lieutenant.

Why am I talking about an old friend? He was a fellow Vietnam Veteran who was cited and recognized for his valor and heroism. He was awarded The Medal of Honor for his service. They renamed the elementary school (Farmedge Elementary) he had attended. It is now the Stephen E. Karopczyc School. In addition, on Saturday, March 10,

2018, members of The American Legion Post 1711 in Levittown, Long Island, NY, unveiled a memorial in his honor – a bronze likeness of Stephen and a plaque to commemorate his significant achievement. Stephen was inducted into the Chaminade Hall of Fame and a Memorial Garden at Springhill College was named in his honor. At the Bethpage train station, there is a memorial to Stephen for his bravery and heroism.

The Virtual Wall (vvmf.org)

Stephen Edward Karopczyc

First Lieutenant

A CO, 2ND BN, 35TH INFANTRY, 25TH INF DIV, USARV

Army of the United States

Bethpage, New York

March 05, 1944, to March 12, 1967

STEPHEN E KAROPCZYC is on the Wall at Panel 16E, Line 69

1LT STEPHEN EDWARD KAROPCZYC

Stephen Edward Karopczyc

Medal of Honor citation:

For conspicuous gallantry and intrepidity in action at the risk of his life above and beyond the call of duty. While leading the 3d Platoon, Company A, on a flanking maneuver against a superior enemy force, 1st Lt. Karopczyc observed that his lead element was engaged with a small enemy unit along his route. Aware of the importance of quickly pushing through to the main enemy force in order to provide relief for a hard-pressed friendly platoon, he dashed through the intense enemy fire into the open and hurled colored smoke grenades to designate the foe for attack by helicopter gunships. He moved among his men to embolden their advance, and he guided their attack by marking enemy locations with bursts of fire from his own weapon. His forceful leadership quickened the advance, forced the enemy to retreat, and allowed his unit to close with the main hostile force. Continuing the deployment of his platoon, he constantly exposed himself as he ran from man to man to give encouragement and to direct their efforts. A shot from an enemy sniper struck him above the heart but he refused aid for this serious injury, plugging the bleeding wound with his finger until it could be properly dressed. As the enemy strength mounted, he ordered his men to organize a defensive position in and around some abandoned bunkers where he conducted a defense against the increasingly strong enemy attacks. After several hours, a North Vietnamese soldier hurled a hand grenade to within a few feet of 1st Lt. Karopczyc and 2 other wounded men. Although his position protected him, he leaped up to cover the deadly grenade with a steel helmet. It exploded to drive fragments into 1st Lt. Karopczyc, but his action prevented further injury to the 2 wounded men. 1st Lt. Karopczyc's heroic leadership, unyielding perseverance, and selfless devotion to his men were directly responsible for the successful and spirited action of his platoon throughout the battle and are in keeping with the highest traditions of the U.S. Army.

1LT STEPHEN EDWARD KAROPCZYC

http://www.virtualwall.org/dk/KaropczycSE01a.htm

ROBERT E SCHOPPAUL
GALE K VOGLER ◆ ROBERT
STEPHEN F BURLINGAME
EDWIN R GOODRICH Jr
STEPHEN E KAROPCZYC
DANNY D RHOADES
FILIBERTO G MIRANDA
TIMOTHY R COX ◆ PAUL
CLARENCE A KIMM ◆ LONNIE
THOMAS R BARRY ◆ VIRGIL B
ANGEL LUIS FRAGOSA-GARCIA
HARRY F CONRAD ◆ GEORGE
ANIBAL DE JESUS SANCHEZ

American Legion Post 1711, Levittown, L.I., NY, includes a memorial plaque dedicated to 1st Lt. Stephen Karopczyc on March 10, 2018.

Stephen's heroism was inspiring. For a lot of people, especially those who were too young to remember Vietnam and even some Vietnam Veterans, reading his Medal of Honor citation will bring a tear to the eye. It does to mine. There's nothing but pride at having known him. My deepest condolences to his family...especially Walter.

As we look at this book and read our own stories, it brings to mind some quotations. One from John Laughlin:

"Many were called, some served, few returned unscathed."

How true. Many Vietnam Veterans don't have physical disabilities or visual wounds, but they've been suffering from flashbacks or PTSD for decades. I can't tell you how often I hear from my fellow Vietnam

Veterans that talking about their war experiences is extremely difficult. I had a classmate from PMC with a unique in country experience. I know readers would've been interested and excited to read about it. But after around six weeks of talking and communicating about his Vietnam War experiences (he even sent some amazing pictures of his unit), he called to tell me he couldn't do it. Recalling what happened in-country was too traumatic.

He was a Navy pilot in a unit providing ground support to Navy Seals, Marines, ARVN, and Army grunts in Southern South Vietnam. It's been over fifty years for some of us but to some, it seems like yesterday.

If mentally and physically able, every Vietnam Veteran should attend a National Vietnam War Veterans Day event on March 29th of every year. Next year, 2023, will be particularly significant – the fiftieth anniversary of the War's end. If possible, plan to attend an event in your area and receive the "Welcome Home" some of us never received. I am proud of my Vietnam Veteran brothers and sisters for their devotion to their service and their country.

SOME STATISTICS ON THE VIETNAM WAR

If you speak to an American who lived through the 50s, 60s and into the early 70s, they are likely to tell you that the Vietnam War was a poor man's war...meaning the undereducated (poorly educated, uneducated, ill-educated, academically challenged, etc.) and people of color served and died at the highest rate. They will say most of those who were KIA were draftees. The statistics shown below will dispel those misconceptions and outline the real facts on the War's impact on its military.

These facts and figures are provided by the Vietnam Veterans of America:

- Vietnam War era: August 1965-May 1973
- U.S. military personnel serving during era – 9,087,000
- Those who served in Southeast Asia Theater – 3,403,000
- Those who served in South Vietnam – 2,594,000
- POW/MIAs – 2,646

- Total casualties – 58, 281
- Severely disabled – 75,000
- Medal of Honor recipients – 258

Here are some stats from the U. S. Government VA website and statisticbrain.com.

- Vietnam Veterans: 9.7% of the population
- Of the 2.6 million who served in Vietnam, between 1-1.6 million (40-60%) fought in combat, provided close support or was at least fairly regularly exposed to enemy attack.
- Peak troop strength in Vietnam: 543,482(April 30,1969)
- Total casualties: 58,281 (See: Chapter 3 – The Wall)
- 8 nurses died
- Married men killed: 17,539
- 61% of the men killed were 21 or younger
- Severely disabled: 75,000 (23,214 – 100% disabled, 5,283 – lost limb, 1,081 – sustained multiple amputations)
- Amputations or crippling wounds to the lower extremities were 300% higher than WWII and 70% higher than Korea. Multiple amputations occurred at the rate of 18.4% compared to 5.7% in WWII.
- Draftees accounted for 30.4% (17,725) of the combat deaths
- Reservists killed:5,977
- National Guard: 6,140 Served; 101 died.
- Religion of dead: Protestant – 64.4%, Roman Catholic – 28.9%, Other/None – 6.7%

Military Make Up

- 25% (648,500) of the total forces in country were draftees
- 76% of the men sent to Vietnam were from lower middle/working class backgrounds.
- 79% of the men who served in Vietnam had a high school education or better when they entered the service (63% of

Korean War Vets and only 45% of WWII Vets completed high school upon separation.)

- 88.4% of the men who actually served in Vietnam were Caucasian, 10.6% were Black, 1% belonged to other races.

Post War Statistics

- 97% of Vietnam Era Veterans were honorably discharged.
- 66% of Vietnam Veterans volunteered.
- 91% of Vietnam Vets say they are glad they served.
- As of 2013, 87% of the public now hold Vietnam Veterans in High esteem – 38 years after the war ended.
- 66% of Vietnam Veterans say they would serve again if called upon.
- 82% of Veterans who saw heavy combat strongly believe and 75% of the public agree the war was a failure of political will not of arms.

AFTERWORD

I hope you now have a better understanding of a time, the Vietnam War, when our nation was in total disarray, and what a terrible time Vietnam Veterans encountered when we can home – disrespect and a lack of support. It didn't matter what branch of the service we were in, we were "guilty."

All four of us would say that most of the men and women we served with were patriotic, hardworking, and trustworthy and always had each other's back. They were dedicated to their work, heroic and focused on achieving their objectives with minimum injuries and/or fatalities. We are proud of them and their service to this country.

When we returned from Vietnam, how many Veterans thought of giving back to their country, i.e., joining VSOs (Veteran Service Organizations), volunteering at a military hospital, visiting local high schools and talking with juniors and seniors during vocation week for a career in the service? How many took advantage of the GI Bill and/or went to college? Tough questions to answer but I'm sure not many of them did these things.

I want to address the Veterans who served in Iraq and/or Afghanistan (or both) post 9/11. Like you, we were young when we came home. We wanted to start a family, to find a career, and to go to college. Our dreams involved saving for the future, getting our life back in order, etc. – just like yours did when you returned from your tour(s). But we came back to a different United States from the one you encountered. You were welcomed with parades. VSOs greeted you at your arrival at the airport. You got to surprise loved ones who didn't know you were coming home. All those things were well-deserved. However, joining a VSO, the American Legion, the VVA, VFW, DAV, and IAVA (Iraq and Afghanistan Veterans of America) wasn't on our radar screens. That's not good.

Many post 9/11 Veterans have returned home suffering from the loss of limbs, disfigurements, PTSD, Traumatic Brain Injuries, burn pit exposure, K2 in Uzbekistan, homelessness, and thoughts of suicide. Getting support from the VA continues to be an ongoing struggle. Let's look at some frightening statistics about suicide among active duty members and Veterans. In an NBC News article dated June 21, 2021, Courtney Kube asserts:

Since 9/11, four times as many U.S. service members and veterans have died by suicide than have been killed in combat, according to a new report. The research, compiled by the Costs of War Project at Brown University, found an estimated 30,177 active duty personnel and veterans who have served in the military since 9/11 have died by suicide, compared with 7,057 killed in post 9/11 military operations.

The President, his/her support of the military, and the competency of the individual in charge of the VA Healthcare System will make all the difference in the type of support you will get. It's not a given.

Leo Shane III drafted an article entitled *Veterans in the 117th Congress, by the Numbers,* which appeared on the Vietnam Veterans of America website dated December 28, 2020. He analyzes the members of this Congress who are Veterans. His conclusion was quite dramatic.

When elected officials gather on Capitol Hill to formally convene the 117th Congress on January 3, they'll do so with 91 veterans among their ranks, the lowest total since at least World War II.

These are the same people (Congress) who will decide on funding the United States military and the VA Healthcare System. Yet they have no experience either in the defense of our country or in taking care of its Veterans, abled or disabled, as they get older. This does not bode well for the post 2001 Veterans. I urge all post-2001 Veterans to join a VSO as soon as possible and to be an active member. The power, strength, and political influence of the VSOs will keep a check on Congress to ensure that the Veteran's benefits we've earned are available, funded, and expanded where necessary. Unfortunately, as we get older, "normal" living becomes harder due to injuries we suffered while we were serving our country.

A perfect example of this is the investigation by the VVA of recent COVID-19 deaths at VA facilities in some states during the pandemic – disgraceful. The American public probably would not have heard about it if it weren't for the VSOs' aggressive investigation.

I am a proud member of The American Legion and a life member of the Vietnam Veterans of America. It doesn't matter which VSO you join, just do it. When I came home from Vietnam, I was told the VSOs were just places where old men and women sat around and ate, drank and told old war stories – true, but only in part.

A VSO *is* a place to meet your brothers and sisters who served in the armed forces and to share experiences. People who did not serve, though well intentioned, simply cannot relate. But VSOs do so much more. Sometimes the public sees the VSO activity in the community, but unfortunately, quite often, their efforts are not publicized and go unseen or unacknowledged.

The VVA has a motto: "Never again will one generation of veterans abandon another."

It is an accurate – and terribly sad – descriptor of what happened to too many returning Vietnam Veterans.

Here is a compelling quotation from an article entitled *Always Valued, Never Forgotten* by General George William Casey, Jr., (USA Ret.) and compiled by Jan C. Scruggs in *A Legacy of Service:*

George Washington is credited with stating that the willingness with which young people are likely to serve in any war will depend on how the veterans of earlier wars were treated and appreciated by their nation.

In February 2021, we lost a beloved WWII Veteran who was 98 years old and a member of our American Legion Post. He was like all our other WWII Veterans who passed since I joined my American Legion Post almost thirteen years ago: the salt of the earth. They were and are proud, patriotic, humble, never bragging about their service or their injuries or the medals they earned. They support the Post whenever possible via donations or participating in events. They stand proudly for the flag even when they have to demand help to get out of their wheelchairs. I am always humbled in their presence, and I am a much better person for having known them. So...

Join a VSO and support our brothers and sisters in arms!

To all the Veterans who read this book and especially my Vietnam brothers and sisters, thank you for your service at a time when you weren't respected, appreciated, or honored when you returned home to America. But, as many WWII Veterans said of their service, you were asked to do a job and you did it. You supported each other and hoped you would see your families again.

To the Lucky Ones who made it home, I hope your life is happy, healthy, loving, and patriotic. May you live a long life under the grace of God.

THANK YOU FOR YOUR SERVICE!

What Is A Veteran?

I developed the following from numerous discussions with my friends, Veterans and non-veterans alike, and hope it sums up a Veteran.

A VETERAN IS...

- A person, male or female, born in the United States (or a naturalized citizen) who has served in a branch of the United States military.
- Someone who comprises less than 8% of the US population.
- A person who enlisted or in time of war was drafted into a branch of the service: Army, Navy, Air Force, Coast Guard, or Marine Corps and who was discharged or released therefrom under conditions other than dishonorable.
- Someone who served his/her country at home or on foreign soil, in the air, or on the sea. The term "service" can be applied to the regular Army, the Reserves or National Guard.
- A person who signed a blank check to his/her country in defending it, saying it is payable in full...including with his/her life.

- Someone who served in either peacetime or in wartime in defense of our country. And wore the uniform with honor, pride, and distinction.
- A patriot who spent time away from family and friends, those who also sacrificed in the serviceperson's commitment to serve their country.
- An individual who lives by the mantra: Duty, Honor, Country.
- A servant who respects his/her leaders, believes in discipline, and follows the chain of command.
- A serviceperson who completes his/her enlistment or military career and returns to civilian life, but still carries the "wounds" of service and who may require the need for further physical and/or mental care.
- Someone who has earned and deserves the respect of every American of every age.

Closing notes.

Close to 30% of Veterans have disabilities.

There is an unbending truth about Veterans: "All gave some, some gave all."

Who do we honor every year on the 11th day of the 11th month and at 1100 hours?

THE VETERAN!

TO THE VIETNAM VETERAN

TO THOSE WHO RETURNED WITH NO ONE TO GREET THEM.

TO THOSE WHO HAVE BEEN TOLD PTSD WOULD GO AWAY IN TIME.

TO THOSE WHO HAVE NEVER BEEN TOLD THANK TOU OR WELCOME HOME.

TO THOSE WHO RETURNED BUT ARE STILL HAUNTED BY THE NIGHTMARES OF WAR.

TO THOSE WHO STILL REACT TO A BACKFIRE AND BREAK A SWEAT AT THE SOUND OF A CHOPPER.

TO THOSE WHO SUFFER FROM AGENT ORANGE EXPOSURE AND ARE STILL FIGHTING THE LAST BATTLE.

TO THOSE WHO FOUGHT BATTLES IN THE JUNGLES OF VIETNAM AND HERE AT HOME.

TO THOSE WHO HAVE MORE FRIENDS ON THE VIETNAM MEMORIAL WALL THAN ALIVE TODAY.

THANK YOU!

A Prayer for Our Veterans

Oh God, Our Heavenly Father,
You have blessed us with
brave men and women
who are willing to defend our freedom.
May Your protection and grace
surround them each day.
Let Your healing hand be upon those
who suffer wounds and injuries.
May those who have made the
ultimate sacrifice rest forever in
Your Holy Presence.
Comfort the families who mourn
and are left to remember
the precious lives of their loved ones.
Help us to honor and support them.
Let us ever be mindful of each sacrifice made
on behalf of the American people by our
sons, daughters, husbands, wives, mothers,
fathers, and friends.
Amen.

About The Authors

KEN BYERLY

Ken grew up in New York before attending and graduating from Pennsylvania Military College. Upon graduation, he married his best friend Jean, had a son and entered the US Army. He was stationed in Germany and Vietnam. He attained the rank of Captain and was awarded the Bronze Star. After the service, Ken spent over 30 years in pharmaceuticals in sales and marketing. He traveled extensively throughout the United States and has lived in six States. Ken and his wife Jean had two grown sons and four grandchildren, ages 9-26 years old. They now are retired and have lived the last 30 years in Ocean City, NJ. Ken and Jean enjoy their family, friends and making trips into Atlantic City for good food and good luck.

JOHN LAUGHLIN

John is a native Philadelphian who spent most of his life in Levittown, PA. He attended Rider University and LaSalle University and holds a degree in Business Administration. He was drafted into the Army in 1966. Then in 1968 he was sent to Vietnam and was wounded during the Tet offensive. John is the proud recipient of the Purple Heart. John resides in Beesleys Point, NJ, with his wife Karen of 50 years. He is the loving father of 3 grown children and 5 grandchildren.

MIKE MORAN

Forty years in manufacturing and finance organizations as a supervisor, manager and director. Married, four children and six grandchildren. Love the beach.

STEVE RAHO

Steve was born in Pottsville, Pennsylvania. He attended Pennsylvania Military College on an ROTC Scholarship. In his Senior Year or as a First Classman, Steve was selected as the Brigade Commander or First Captain of the Corps of Cadets. Upon graduation, Steve entered the U. S. Army as a second lieutenant and spent almost the next 30 years as a highly decorated career officer and retired as a Full Colonel. Steve served in multiple bases in the US, in Vietnam and Korea in a variety of positions. When he retired from the service, Steve was hired by the Department of the Army to serve as the Director, Army Records Management & Declassification Agency. Some of Steve's military awards and decorations include the Combat Infantryman's Badge or CIB, four Legions of Merit, Bronze Star, six Meritorious Service Medals, nine Air Medals, two Army Commendation Medals and more.

Steve and his wife, Sheila, are now retired and living in Virginia.

Endnotes

Chapter 1

1. U.S. Government (VA Website stats), "The Veterans Hour." ArmedForcesPress.com/, 2013 MEDIA EDITION) and the statisticbrain.com web site from 2014:

Printed in the USA
CPSIA information can be obtained
at www.ICGtesting.com
LVHW020016170124
769072LV00046B/1858